The Seven Deadly Sins

The Seven Deadly Sins
A Companion

Ronnie S. Landau

Copyright © 2010 by Ronnie S. Landau

All rights reserved. No part of this book may be reproduced, stored, or transmitted by any means—whether auditory, graphic, mechanical, or electronic—without written permission of both publisher and author, except in the case of brief excerpts used in critical articles and reviews. Unauthorized reproduction of any part of this work is illegal and is punishable by law.

ISBN: 978-1-4457-3227-5

Contents

INTRODUCTION 1

LUST 9

GLUTTONY...29

SLOTH...45

GREED...63

WRATH 81

ENVY...97

PRIDE 115

INTRODUCTION

The Bible and several other self-help or enlightenment books cite the Seven Deadly Sins. They are: pride, greed, lust, envy, wrath, sloth, and gluttony. That pretty much covers everything that we do, that is sinful... or fun for that matter.

Dave Mustaine
(lead guitarist, songwriter and vocalist for the
American heavy metal band Megadeth).

The Seven Deadly Sins: their 'Appeal' and Significance

Let's face it: sin is more fascinating and appealing than virtue. This explains why *The National Enquirer* sells in greater numbers than *The Church Times* – and why reports of crimes and the frailties of human nature, rather than spiritually uplifting stories of kindness and charity, dominate the TV news headlines. More words have been written and books sold on the subject of Adolf Hitler than on any other historical figure; sadly, he is bigger 'box office' than Winston Churchill, Elvis Presley and Mother Teresa put together.

It should therefore come as no surprise to discover that, over the centuries, poets, philosophers, humourists, playwrights, Hollywood moguls, statesmen, theologians, artists, psychologists and dictionary compilers have had so much to say on the subject of this book. It has also given professed lovers of goodness the excuse to tub-thump, pontificate and generally patronise the rest of us, while at the same time pretending to be shocked and offended by the excesses to which those of us, who are caught – however fleetingly - in the grip of one or more of these vices, are drawn. On a deeply subconscious level, the many unwitting contributors to this collection of quotations, are perhaps merely projecting their own guilt, shame, predilections and, for all I know, unfulfilled fantasies onto the target of their scathing and, often, witty attack.

In truth, they are morally no better than those hypocritical journalists at the UK *News of the World* or *Sunday People* who, as they tease and titillate their readers, feign outrage and indignation at the profligacy and licentiousness of the central characters of their stories. But, whatever their hidden motives and secret passions, all strength to them: for their pithy observations are the very lifeblood of this book!

Now, I don't wish to speculate on the possible origin of the Christian Church's fixation on blood, sin, temptation, and sexual 'depravity', except to say that it would surely take a battalion of shrinks several years to come up with competing explanations of a decidedly psycho-pathological bent! On the other hand, when one looks at the broad sweep of history, maybe all religion has just been an unbelievably popular and socially acceptable form of OCD (Obsessive-compulsive Disorder).

The three-word term 'Seven Deadly Sins' is a superbly effective and memorable catch-phrase - a 21st-century copywriter or 'branding' guru could not better it. Each word is truly powerful. Working backwards, the word 'Sin(s)' holds a profound and enduring fascination for us all. Although many of us would today have a purely secular understanding of the term, 'sin' is used mainly in a religious context to describe an act that violates a moral rule, and each of the major religions has a distinctive take on the meaning of the term.

INTRODUCTION 3

The word 'Deadly' evokes the morbid preoccupation, spoken and unspoken, that we all have with death. Why, after all, does every other television drama and Hollywood movie seem to be concerned with murder, whether of the individual or, increasingly, of the 'serial' variety? In their British form, these productions frequently involve murders committed in the unlikeliest of peaceful rural settings, while, in their American version, they generally occur in the urban contexts of Los Angeles, San Francisco, Chicago or New York. Use of the term 'Deadly' also reminds us that we are all subject to the laws of mortality: rock stars, dustmen, football icons, teachers and royalty alike. Moreover, with reference to the Seven Deadly Sins, the early church had a very specific theological understanding of the word 'Deadly'.

As for 'Seven', over the ages this number has proved of immense significance, psychologically, culturally and religiously. Ask 100 people to make an instant choice of a number between one and ten and well over half will, it has been proved, choose Seven. There were, of course, Seven Wonders of the World (the ancient world) and there are now Seven new ones recently voted into existence on the internet. The ancient world also gave us the Seven Planets and the Seven Ages of Man. 'Seven Brides for Seven Brothers' was a Hollywood blockbuster, as was the more recent serial killer movie 'Se7en'. 'The Seventh Seal' was an Ingmar Bergman classic, and who has not seen 'The Magnificent Seven' or its Japanese progenitor 'The Seven Samurai'? Snow White had her Seven Dwarfs, while 'Lucky Number Slevin' was another successful movie. Mariners sail the Seven seas, Seven Dials is a fashionable shopping area in London's Covent Garden, while David Beckham's England shirt proudly boasts the number 7 - as, indeed, did George Best's Manchester United and Stanley Matthews' own England shirts.

4   *The Seven Deadly Sins*

'The Secret Seven' was a famous children's novel by Enid Blyton, and 'Blake's 7' a popular BBC Science Fiction series in the late 70s. '7 Up' is not only an internationally renowned soft drink, but was also the title of a groundbreaking series of TV programmes, with a new chapter every Seven years, examining various social factors in human development by following a group of children, later adults, from radically different social and cultural backgrounds. The starting point for the title was the Jesuit promise (threat?) of indoctrination, 'Give me a child until it is Seven and I will show you the man'. On an even more depressing note, the London bombings were on 7/7 (not just a coincidence, mouth the doomsayers).

And we're not finished yet! Husbands and wives experience the 'Seven-year Itch', there were, and are, Seven hills in Rome (The Aventine, Caelian, Capitoline, Esquiline, Palatine, Quirinal and Viminal), and if you break a mirror it is, of course, Seven years' bad luck. And, let's not forget, secret agent James Bond is 00<u>7</u>.

In Judaism, the number Seven is of unparalleled numerical and numerological significance. The Lord created the world in six days and, on the Seventh, rested. So the *Shabbat* (Sabbath), that Seventh day, became the holiest day of the Jewish week. So the number Seven became connected with the idea of perfection. Each of our own weeks consequently has Seven days. In Jewish liturgy, at the climax to *Yom Kippur* (The Day of Atonement), the most sacred day in the Jewish calendar, congregants repeat the incantation 'The Lord, He is our God' Seven times.

Seven is a highly symbolic number in the *Torah* (Jewish bible), referring to the infusion of spirituality and Godliness into the Creation. Hence 'Shiva' (another pronunciation of the Hebrew word for Seven) is the number of days of mourning. Hence, the mourner *sits Shiva*. The weekly *Torah* portion is divided into Seven sections, and Seven men or boys over the age of 13 are 'called up' for the reading of these excerpts during *Shabbat* morning services. Seven blessings are recited under the *chuppah* (wedding canopy) during a Jewish wedding ceremony and the bride circles her husband Seven times. A Jewish bride and groom are feted with Seven days of festive meals after their wedding, known as *Sheva Berachot* ("Seven Blessings"). The *menorah* was a Seven-branched candelabrum lit by olive oil in the Tabernacle and the Temple in Jerusalem. The *menorah* is one of the oldest symbols of the Jewish people. It is said to represent the burning bush as seen by Moses on Mount Sinai.

The number Seven similarly had great prominence within the early and medieval Christian church. The Seven Deadly Sins became one of a number of important groups of Seven: the Seven Canonical Hours, the Seven Petitions of the Lord's Prayer, The Seven Joys and Seven Sorrows of the Virgin and the Seven Corporal Works of Mercy and Seven Spiritual Acts of Mercy. Later Christianity drew attention to the Seven Signs (of Christ's divinity) in St John's Gospel, the Seven Churches in the Book of Revelations, the Seven Last Words (of Jesus) from the Cross, the Seven Sacraments in the Christian faith (though some traditions assign a different number), the Seven terraces of Mount Purgatory (one per deadly sin) and the Seven Virtues: chastity, moderation, liberality, charity, meekness, zeal, and humility (expressed slightly differently in the table below).

A Brief History

The concept of the Seven Deadly Sins appears to owe its origin to St John Cassian (360-435), who first identified them. They were then refined by Pope Gregory the Great (540 - 604), whom most scholars believe to have been the true author.

6   *The Seven Deadly Sins*

In the late 6th century, Pope Gregory the Great had ranked the Sins in order of seriousness, based on the degree to which they offended against love. In his view, it was, from the most serious to the least: pride, envy, anger, sadness, avarice, gluttony, and lust. Later theologians, including St. Thomas Aquinas, would contradict the notion that the seriousness of the sins could be ranked in this way.

By the seventeenth century the church had replaced the original vague term 'sadness' (*tristitia*) with 'sloth' (*acedia*). While there has, since then, been agreement on which sins constitute the Seven, there seems to have been no reliable consensus on their correct order. However, the table opposite lists The Seven Deadly Sins (vices) in one of the more traditional orders in which they have appeared since then (in the main quotations section of the book I shall be treating them in reverse order). And just so you are absolutely clear next time you feel an attack of vice coming on, the virtues against which they sin are also provided.

They are contrasted in this table with the contrary virtues against which they sin. (While the list itself is not strictly biblical, the Bible forbids all seven in various places.)

The Latin equivalent is given in italics:

VICE	VIRTUE AGAINST WHICH IT SINS
Pride *Superbia*	Humility
Envy *Invidia*	Love and Kindness
Wrath/Anger *Ira*	Kindness
Avarice/ Greed *Avaritia*	Charity
Sloth *Acedia*	Diligence
Gluttony *Gula*	Temperance
Lust *Luxuria*	Self control and chastity

These 'sins' were called 'deadly' since the church drew a distinction between sins which were 'venial' (from the Latin *venia = pardon)*, and could be forgiven without the need for the sacrament of Confession and those which were 'capital' and merited damnation, eternal or otherwise. Capital or Deadly Sins were held to have a fatal effect on an individual's spiritual health. For example, medieval wall paintings emphasized the

8   *The Seven Deadly Sins*

sequential link between the commission of a deadly sin and one being sent to Hell.

The Seven Deadly Sins, also known as 'mortal sins', 'capital vices' or 'cardinal sins' are a classification of vices that were originally used in early Christian teachings to educate and instruct followers concerning 'fallen' man's tendency to sin. Beginning in the early 14th century, the popularity of the Seven Deadly Sins as a theme among European artists eventually helped to inculcate them in many areas of Christian society and culture throughout the world. One means of such embedding was the invention in the early modern period of the mnemonic 'SALIGIA', based on the first letters in Latin of the sins: *Superbia, Avaritia, Luxuria, Invidia, Gula, Ira, Acedia.*

In case you were beginning to wonder whether all this might be irrelevant to the modern world, the Vatican has recently announced an up-to-date list - 1,500 years after the Catholic Church came up with the original Seven – to keep pace with our changing contemporary world.

The new sins are:

1) Genetic modification;
2) Human experimentations;
3) Polluting the environment;
4) Social injustice;
5) Causing poverty;
6) Financial gluttony;
7) Taking drugs.

LUST
(Latin, *luxuria*)

Lust is an enemy to the purse, a foe to the person, a canker to the mind, a corrosive to the conscience, a weakness of the wit, a besotter of the senses, and finally, a mortal bane to all the body.

Pliny the Elder

Since the sexual revolution of the 1960s, sex is ubiquitous, and lust certainly appears less 'sinful' than it had hitherto been. Sex is now used to sell just about everything: chocolate, alcohol, clothing, books, air travel, movies, fragrances, music, automobiles - you name it, sex sells it. In other words, man's (and woman's) potential for lustful feelings are today exploited rather than denied, hidden or discouraged.

Sex may now be out in the open, but traditionally the sexual realm was considered very private. Lust was – and still often is - thought of as involving excessive or compulsive sexual thoughts which can be destructive of the individual, of the family and of society itself. Unfulfilled lustful appetites can lead to anti-social behaviour such as sexual addiction, adultery, rape or even incest. In the medieval period, Dante's definition of lust was "excessive love of others," which consequently relegated devotion to God to a lesser status. Similarly the Bible's injunction against idol worship (one of the Ten

Commandments) is interpreted by some modern Biblical scholars as warning against an over-enthusiastic (or unhealthy) devotion to anything other than God. That would embrace any addiction, be it to sex, drugs or even television.

A non-sexual relationship is commonly termed 'Platonic' because the Greek philosopher Plato believed that, in the struggle within the individual human soul, 'reason' should triumph over the 'appetites'. And the three basic human appetites are for food, sex and power.

I have included some quotations that see lust as not being restricted to the 'sexual' realm: the lust for power and conquest, for example.

>>>

LUST

The war between the sexes is the only one in which both sides regularly sleep with the enemy.

Quentin Crisp

***

God gave men both a penis and a brain, but unfortunately not enough blood supply to run both at the same time.

Robin Williams

***

Behind every successful man you'll find a woman who has nothing to wear.

Harold Coffin

***

I am going to say this again: I did not have sexual relations with that woman, Miss Lewinsky.

William Jefferson (Bill) Clinton

***

Sex – it's the best fun I've ever had without smiling.

Woody Allen

***

A hard dog to keep on the porch.

Hillary Clinton (on her husband's extra-marital activities)

***

Lust is the craving for salt of a man who is dying of thirst.

Frederick Buechner

***

As pills that are outwardly fair, gilt, and rolled in sugar, but within are full of bitterness: even so lustful pleasure is no sooner hatched but repentance is at hand, ready to supplant her.

Daniel Cawdrey

***

If venereal delight and the power of propagating the species were permitted only to the virtuous, it would make the world very good.

James Boswell

***

Ambition is a lust that is never quenched, but grows more inflamed and madder by enjoyment.

Thomas Otway

***

Sex without love is an empty experience, but, as empty experiences go, it's one of the best.

Woody Allen

***

LUST 13

Servile inclinations, and gross love,
 The guilty bent of vicious appetite;
 At first a sin, a horror ev'n in bliss,
 Deprave the senses and lay waste the man;
 Passions irregular, and next a loathing,
 Quickly succeed to dash the wild.

William Havard

***

Nature is content with little; grace with less; but lust with nothing.

Matthew (Mathew) Henry

***

Clinton lied. A man might forget where he parks or where he lives, but never forgets oral sex, no matter how bad it is.

Barbara Bush

***

I know the very difference that lies 'twixt hallowed love and base unholy lust; I know the one is as a golden spur, urging the spirit to all noble aims; the other but a foul and miry pit, o'erthrowing it in midst of its career.

Frances Anne "Fanny" Kemble (Mrs. Butler)

***

14   *The Seven Deadly Sins*

Capricious, wanton, bold, and brutal Lust
   Is meanly selfish; when resisted, cruel;
   And, like the blast of Pestilential Winds,
   Taints the sweet bloom of Nature's fairest forms.

John Milton

***

In the sex-war thoughtlessness is the weapon of the male, vindictiveness of the female.

Cyril Connolly

***

Lust is, of all the frailties of our nature, what most we ought to fear; the headstrong beast rushes along, impatient of the course; nor hears the rider's call, nor feels the rein.

Nicholas Rowe

***

The only safe pleasure for a parliamentarian is a bag of boiled sweets.

Julian Critchley

***

LUST   15

Among men, sex sometimes results in intimacy; among women, intimacy sometimes results in sex.

Barbara Cartland

***

An enemy to whom you show kindness becomes your friend, excepting lust, the indulgence of which increases its enmity.

Moslih Eddin

***

When turkeys mate they think of swans.

Johnny Carson

***

Lust is a captivity of the reason and an enraging of the passions. It hinders business and distracts counsel. It sins against the body and weakens the soul.

Jeremy Taylor

***

The good thing about masturbation is that you don't have to dress up for it.

Truman Capote

***

16   *The Seven Deadly Sins*

The human spirit sublimates the impulses it thwarts; a healthy sex life mitigates the lust for other sports.

Piet Hein

***

The true feeling of sex is that of a deep intimacy, but above all of a deep complicity.

James Dickey

***

Remember, if you smoke after sex you're doing it too fast.

Woody Allen

***

Lust is a vice sooner condemned than banished; easily spoke against, but yet it will fawn as smoothly on our flesh as Circe on the Graecian travelers, when she detained them in the shape of beasts.

W. Mason

***

Clinton had sex with loads of women and had only one war. Bush has stuck with his wife and had loads of wars. Draw your own conclusions.

Michael Ehioze Ediae

***

LUST   17

But when Lust
    By unchaste looks, loose gestures, and foul talk,
    But most by lewd and lavish arts of sin,
    Lets in defilement to the inward parts,
    The soul grows clotted by contagion,
    Imbodies and imbrutes, till she quite lose
    The divine property of her first being.

John Milton

***

An orgasm a day keeps the doctor away.

Mae West

***

I never resist temptation, because I have found that things that are bad for me do not tempt me.

George Bernard Shaw

***

So long as lust (whether of the world or flesh) smells sweet in our nostrils, so long we are loathesome to God.

Charles Caleb Colton

***

They don't call me 'Tyrannosaurus Sex' for nothing.

Edward Kennedy

***

18   *The Seven Deadly Sins*

How love the limb-loosener sweeps me away.

Sappho

***

No place, no company, no age, no person is temptation-free; let no man boast that he was never tempted, let him not be high-minded, but fear, for he may be surprised in that very instant wherein he boasteth that he was never tempted at all.

Herbert Spencer

***

It depends on what the meaning of the word 'is' is.

Bill Clinton

***

His finest hour lasted a minute and a half.

Phyllis Diller

***

I lose my respect for the man who can make the mystery of sex the subject of a coarse jest, yet when you speak earnestly and seriously on the subject, is silent.

Henry David Thoreau

***

LUST   19

I never miss a chance to have sex or appear on television.

Gore Vidal

***

What is peculiar to modern societies is not that they consigned sex to a shadow existence, but that they dedicated themselves to speaking of it ad infinitum, while exploiting it as the secret.

Michel Foucault

***

An orgasm is just a reflex, like a sneeze.

Ruth Westheimer

***

If I don't have a woman every three days or so, I get a terrible headache.

John Fitzgerald Kennedy

***

I think making love is the best form of exercise.

Cary Grant (Archibald Alec Leach)

***

The real theatre of the sex war is the domestic hearth.

Germaine Greer

***

You mustn't force sex to do the work of love or love to do the work of sex.

Mary McCarthy

***

A bachelor has to have inspiration for making love to a woman, a married man needs only an excuse.

Helen Rowland

***

Sex hasn't been the same since women started enjoying it.

Lewis Grizzard

***

Nobody will ever win the battle of the sexes. There's too much fraternizing with the enemy.

Henry Kissinger

***

Temptations, like misfortunes, are sent to test our moral strength.

Marguerite de Valois

***

LUST   21

The only way to get rid of a temptation is to yield to it.

Oscar Wilde

***

The drive to propagate our race has also propagated a lot of other things.

Georg Christoph Lichtenberg

***

I'm suggesting we call sex something else, and it should include everything from kissing to sitting close together.

Shere Hite

***

'Tis one thing to be tempted, another thing to fall.

William Shakespeare

***

I've looked on so many women with lust. I've committed adultery in my heart many times. God knows I will do this and forgives me.

Jimmy Carter

***

Sex is a discovery.

Fannie Hurst

***

Sex appeal is fifty percent what you've got and fifty percent what people think you've got.

Sophia Loren

***

The blood of youth burns not with such excess as gravity's revolt to wantonness.

William Shakespeare

***

Sex is hardly ever just about sex.

Shirley MacLaine

***

Sex is an emotion in motion.

Mae West

***

Lust is to the other passions what the nervous fluid is to life; it supports them all, lends strength to them all ambition, cruelty, avarice, revenge, are all founded on lust.

Marquis de Sade

***

However muted its present appearance may be, sexual domination obtains nevertheless as perhaps the most pervasive ideology of our culture and provides its most fundamental concept of power.

Kate Millett

***

It is not sex that gives the pleasure, but the lover.

Marge Piercy

***

We throw the whole drudgery of creation on one sex, and then imply that no female of any delicacy would initiate any effort in that direction.

George Bernard Shaw

***

Nothing is either all masculine or all feminine except having sex.

Marlo Thomas

***

The last time I was inside a woman was when I went on a visit to the Statue of Liberty.

Woody Allen

***

I'm all for bringing back the birch, but only between consenting adults.

Gore Vidal

***

Sex is the biggest nothing of all time.

Andy Warhol

***

Healthy, lusty sex is wonderful.

John Wayne

***

Lust's passion will be served; it demands, it militates, it tyrannizes.

Marquis de Sade

***

When tempted to be unfaithful, the intellectual woman will try to inspire her husband with indifference, the sentimental woman with hatred, and the passionate woman with disgust.

Honore de Balzac

***

LUST   25

Whether we fall by ambition, blood, or lust, like diamonds we are cut with our own dust.

John Webster

***

Virtue, as it never will be moved,
    Though Lewdness court it in a shape of Heav'n;
    So Lust, though to a radiant angel link'd,
    Will sate itself in a celestial bed,
    And prey on garbage.

William Shakespeare

***

Why comes temptation but for man to meet
    And master and make crouch beneath his foot,
    And so be pedestaled in triumph?

Robert Browning

***

Whoever lives looking for pleasure only, his senses uncontrolled, immoderate in his enjoyments, idle and weak, the tempter will certainly overcome him, as the wind blows down a weak tree.

Buddha (Gautama Buddha)

***

Temptation is a fearful word. It indicates the beginning of a possible series of infinite evils. It is the ringing of an alarm bell, whose melancholy sounds may reverberate through eternity. Like the sudden, sharp cry of "Fire!" under our windows by night, it should rouse us to instantaneous action, and brace every muscle to its highest tension.

Horace Mann

***

St. Augustine teaches us that there is in each man a Serpent, an Eve, and an Adam. Our senses and natural propensities are the Serpent; the excitable desire is the Eve; and reason is the Adam. Our nature tempts us perpetually; criminal desire is often excited; but sin is not completed till reason consents.

Blaise Pascal

***

Sex between a man and a woman can be wonderful, provided you can get between the right man and the right woman.

Woody Allen

***

Variety, multiplicity are the two most powerful vehicles of lust.

Marquis de Sade

***

Lust is what keeps you wanting to do it even when you have no desire to be with each other. Love is what makes you want to be with each other even when you have no desire to do it.

Judith Viorst

***

The flesh being proud, Desire doth fight with Grace,
    For there it revels, and when that decays,
    The guilty Rebel for remission prays.

William Shakespeare

***

To attempt to resist temptation, to abandon our bad habits, and to control our dominant passions in our own unaided strength, is like attempting to check by a spider's thread the progress of a ship of the first rate, borne along before wind and tide.

Benjamin Waugh

***

I will far rather see the race of man extinct than that we should become less than beasts by making the noblest of God's creation, woman, the object of our lust.

Mohandas Gandhi

***

The most violent appetites in all creatures are lust and hunger; the first is a perpetual call upon them to propagate their kind, the latter to preserve themselves.

Joseph Addison

***

Love begins with an image; lust with a sensation.

Mason Cooley

***

There is a lust in man no charm can tame: Of loudly publishing his neighbour's shame: On eagles wings immortal scandals fly, while virtuous actions are born and die.

William Harvey

***

A fascist is one whose lust for money or power is combined with such an intensity of intolerance toward those of other races, parties, classes, religions, cultures, regions or nations, as to make him ruthless in his use of deceit or violence to attain his ends.

Henry A. Wallace

***

Though lust do masque in ne'er so strange disguise she's oft found witty, but is never wise.

John Webster

***

GLUTTONY
(Latin, *gula*)

Gluttony is an emotional escape, a sign something is eating us.

Peter de Vries

Gluttony, the over-indulgence or over-consumption of anything to the point of waste, could be said to be the curse of the modern age. In our environmentally conscious times it can be seen not only to harm the 'sinner' but to do untold damage to countless others, including billions yet to be born: for the by-product of excessive consumption is ecological disaster. Whilst our now fashionable recycling of waste products may indeed salvage our consciences, in the battle to heal the planet it is not entirely unlike spitting into the wind.

Derived from the Latin verb *gluttire*, meaning to swallow or gulp down, gluttony - the excessive desire for food – was, in medieval Christian thought, considered to lead inevitably to its being withheld from the needy and was therefore deemed a sin. Whether the full larders, bulging refrigerators, butter mountains and wine lakes of today's developed world are, to an extent, conditional upon and responsible for the empty bellies in so much of the rest of the world is a moot point, best left to experts in the economics of globalisation.

Closely related to gluttony is the problem of obesity. Obesity is today one of the leading preventable causes of death throughout the world, with increasing prevalence among both adults and especially children. Authorities view it as one of the most serious public health problems of the 21st century. Obesity may be stigmatized in the modern western world, though at other times in history it has been perceived as a symbol of wealth and fertility, and still is in many parts of Africa.

>>>

More die in the United States of too much food than of too little.

J. K. Galbraith

***

My doctor told me to stop having intimate dinners for four - unless there are three other people.

Orson Welles

***

A gourmet who thinks of calories is like a tart who looks at her watch.

James Beard

***

Gluttony is the source of all our infirmities, and the fountain of all our diseases. As a lamp is choked by a superabundance of oil, a fire extinguished by excess of fuel, so is the natural health of the body destroyed by intemperate diet.

Robert Burton

***

Glutton: one who digs his grave with his teeth.

French Proverb

***

32   *The Seven Deadly Sins*

A big man is always accused of gluttony, whereas a wizened or osseous man can eat like a refugee at every meal, and no one ever notices his greed.

Robertson Davies

***

To lengthen thy life, lessen thy meals.

Benjamin Franklin

***

Gluttony hinders chastity.

Pope Xystus I

***

Gluttony kills more than the sword and is the kindliest of all evils.

Patricius

***

He was a kind and thankful toad, whose heart dilated in proportion as his skin was filled with good cheer; and whose spirits rose with eating, as some men's do with drink.

Washington Irving

***

Gluttony and drunkenness have two evils attendant on them; they make the carcass smart, as well as the pocket.

Marcus Aurelius

***

Swinish gluttony never looks to heaven amidst its gorgeous feast; but with besotted, base ingratitude, cravens and blasphemes his feeder.

John Milton

***

The belly has no ears.

Plutarch

***

But for the cravings of the belly not a bird would have fallen into the snare; nay, nay, the fowler would not have spread his net. The belly is chains to the hands and fetters to the feet. He who is a slave to his belly seldom worships God.

Moslih Eddin

***

Such, whose sole bliss is eating, who can give but that one brutal reason why they live.

Juvenal

***

Born merely for the purpose of digestion.

Jean de la Bruyere

***

Some men find happiness in gluttony and in drunkenness, but no delicate viands can touch their taste with the thrill of pleasure, and what generosity there is in wine steadily refuses to impart its glow to their shriveled hearts.

Edwin Percy Whipple

***

In love, as in gluttony, pleasure is a matter of the utmost precision.

Italo Calvino

***

It is the just doom of laziness and gluttony to be inactive without ease and drowsy without tranquillity.

Samuel Johnson

***

They are sick that surfeit with too much, as they that starve with nothing.

William Shakespeare

***

Gluttony is not a secret vice.

Orson Welles

GLUTTONY   35

Why, at this rate, a fellow that has but a groat in his pocket may have a stomach capable of a ten-shilling ordinary.

William Congreve

***

A gourmet is just a glutton with brains.

Philip W. Haberman, Jr.

***

As houses well stored with provisions are likely to be full of mice, so the bodies of those that eat much are full of diseases.

Laertius Diogenes

***

The inferior creatures groan under your cruelties. You hunt them for your pleasure, and overwork them for your covetousness, and kill them for your gluttony, and set them to fight one with another till they die, and count it a sport and a pleasure to behold them worry one another.

Thomas Tryon

***

Obesity is not gluttony.

George Blackburn

***

36   *The Seven Deadly Sins*

If America can go to the moon, then in the decades to come we should not ever have to have young Americans sent to any part of the world to defend and die for America's gluttony on fossil fuel.

Senator John Kerry

***

The ass bears the load, but not the overload.

Cervantes

***

The body, too, with, yesterday's excess
   Burden'd and tired shall the pure soul depress;
   Weigh down this portion of celestial birth,
   The breath of God, and fix it to the earth.

Horace

***

Of what delights are we deprived by our excesses!

Joseph Joubert

***

When I behold a fashionable table set out in all its magnificence, I fancy that I see gouts and dropsies, fevers and lethargies, with other innumerable distempers lying in ambuscade among the dishes. Nature delights in the most plain and simple diet. Every animal but man keeps to one dish. Herbs are the food of this species, fish of that, and flesh of a third. Man falls upon everything that comes in his way; not the smallest fruit or excrescence of the earth, scarce a berry or a mushroom can escape him.

Joseph Addison

***

Allow not nature more than nature needs.

William Shakespeare

***

Most persons are disposed to expend more than they can afford, and to indulge more than they can endure.

Madame Marie Madeleine Puisieux

***

He who indulges his sense in any excesses renders himself obnoxious to his own reason; and, to gratify the brute in him, displeases the man, and sets his two natures at variance.

Sir Walter Scott

***

He that prolongs his meals, and sacrifices his time as well as his other conveniences, to his luxury, how quickly does he outset his pleasure!

Bishop Robert South

***

38   *The Seven Deadly Sins*

It is a curious fact that no man likes to call himself a glutton, and yet each of us has in him a trace of gluttony, potential or actual. I cannot believe that there exists a single coherent human being who will not confess, at least to himself, that once or twice he has stuffed himself to bursting point on anything from quail financiere to flapjacks, for no other reason than the beastlike satisfaction of his belly.

M.F.K. Fisher

***

All the crimes on earth do not destroy so many of the human race, nor alienate so much property, as drunkenness.

Francis Bacon

***

I am a great eater of beef, and I believe that does harm to my wit.

William Shakespeare

***

He who distinguishes the true savour of his food can never be a glutton; he who does not cannot be otherwise.

Henry David Thoreau

***

O gluttony, it is to thee we owe our griefs!

Geoffrey Chaucer

***

GLUTTONY 39

The casuists have classed gluttony as one of the seven deadly sins, but if it is not tainted by the vice of drinking to inebriation or eating to excess, it deserves to be on a par with the theological virtues.

Lucien Tendret

***

I am not a glutton — I am an explorer of food.

Erma Bombeck

***

Our fear of hypocrisy is forcing us to live in a world where gluttons are fine, so long as they champion gluttony.

Jonah Goldberg

***

If a man get a fever, or a pain in the head with over-drinking, we are subject to curse the wine, when we should rather impute it to ourselves for the excess.

Desiderius Gerhard Erasmus

***

Every morsel to a satisfied hunger is only a new labor to a tired digestion.

Bishop Robert South

***

40   *The Seven Deadly Sins*

The flesh endures the storms of the present alone; the mind, those of the past and future as well as the present. Gluttony is a lust of the mind.

Thomas Hobbes

***

And by his side rode loathsome gluttony.
    Deform'd creature, on a filthy swine;
    His belly was up-blown with luxury,
    And eke with fatness swollen were his eyne.

Edmund Spenser

***

As for me, give me turtle or give me death. What is life without turtle? Nothing. What is turtle without life? Nothinger still.

Artemus Ward (pseudonym of Charles Farrar Browne)

***

Ever a glutton, at another's cost,
    But in whose kitchen dwells perpetual frost.

John Dryden

***

What I like about gluttony,' a bishop I knew used to say, 'is that it doesn't hurt anyone else'.

Monica Furlong

***

GLUTTONY 41

A surfeit of the sweetest things
  The deepest loathing to the stomach brings.

William Shakespeare

***

Eat slowly; only men in rags
  and gluttons old in sin
  Mistake themselves for carpet-bags
  And tumble victuals in.

Sir Walter Raleigh

***

When gourmandism turns into gluttony, voracity, or perversion, it loses its name, its attributes, and all of its meaning, and becomes fit subject for the moralist who can preach upon it or the doctor who can cure it with his prescriptions.

Jean-Antheleme Brillat-Savarin

***

The miser and the glutton are two
  facetious buzzards: one hides his
  store, and the other stores his hide.

Josh Billings

***

42　　*The Seven Deadly Sins*

This is the artist, then, life's hungry man, the
　　glutton of eternity, beauty's miser, glory's slave.

Thomas Wolfe

***

Not addicted to gluttony or drunkenness, this people who incur
no expense in food or dress, and whose minds are always bent
upon the defence of their country, and on the means of plunder,
are wholly employed in the care of their horses and furniture.

Giraldus Cambrensis

***

Let me have men about me that are fat; sleek-headed men, and
such as sleep o' nights; yonder Cassius has a lean and hungry
look; he thinks too much; such men are dangerous.

William Shakespeare

***

Gluttony is a great fault; but we do not necessarily dislike a
glutton. We only dislike the glutton when he becomes a
gourmet--that is, we only dislike him when he not only wants
the best for himself, but knows what is best for other people.

G.K. Chesterton

***

In general, mankind, since the improvement of cookery, eats twice as much as nature requires.

Benjamin Franklin

***

The fool that eats till he is sick
  must fast till he is well.

George W. Thornbury

***

Socrates said, "Bad men live that they may eat and drink, whereas good men eat and drink that they may live."

Plutarch

***

The glutton is much more than an animal and much less than a man.

Honore de Balzac

***

44   *The Seven Deadly Sins*

SLOTH
(Latin, *acedia*)

Well, we can't stand around here doing nothing, people will think we're workmen.

Spike Milligan

Whereas in its original medieval conception sloth was seen as a kind of spiritual apathy, a dereliction of religious duty, especially a failure to appreciate and respond to the world God had created, nowadays it would be viewed as laziness, under-achievement, a failure, through idleness, to realise one's potential.

The modern interpretation of this vice would also point up indifference and passivity, especially the failure to act in order to prevent injustice - more a sin of omission than of commission. In much of the literature on the Nazi Holocaust, for example, the passive bystander is almost as much a player on the historical stage as the perpetrator and the victim (see the first quotation, from Ian Kershaw). As one historian put it, in a memorable three-point prohibition, the lessons of the Holocaust for humanity are, quite simply: 'Do not be a perpetrator; do not be a victim; and do not be a bystander'.

The seemingly endless capacity for boredom among the young (and the not-so-young), surrounded as they are by ever more sophisticated modern gadgetry, and the inability and unwillingness to create one's own entertainment, are features of late twentieth-century and early twenty-first century life; they are also, I would argue, contemporary forms of sloth.

To a greater extent than is the case with the other six sins, the definition of sloth has changed radically since its original inclusion among the seven deadly sins. In fact, it was originally called the sin of 'sadness' (Latin *tristitia*), the joyless refusal to take any pleasure in the world God had created.

SLOTH   47

The road to Auschwitz was built on the savage hatred of only a few, but it was paved with the indifference of many.

Ian Kershaw

***

Sloth is an inlet to disorder, and makes way for licentiousness.. People that have nothing to do are quickly tired of their own company.

Jeremy Collier

***

The very soul of the slothful does effectually but lie drowsing in his body, and the whole man is totally given up to his senses.

Sir Roger L'Estrange

***

Lost time is never found again.

James H. Aughey

***

Every man is, or hopes to be, an idler.

Samuel Johnson

***

He is not only idle who does nothing, but he is idle who might
be better employed.

Socrates

***

I need so much time for doing nothing that I have no time for
work.

Pierre Reverdy

***

I was raised to feel that doing nothing was a sin. I had to learn to
do nothing.

Jenny Joseph

***

Sloth makes all things difficult, but industry all easy; and he that
riseth late must trot all day, and shall scarce overtake his
business at night; while laziness travels so slowly that poverty
soon overtakes him.

Benjamin Franklin

***

To do nothing at all is the most difficult thing in the world, the
most difficult and the most intellectual.

Oscar Wilde

***

Thus idly busy rolls their world away.

Oliver Goldsmith

***

To do nothing is sometimes a good remedy.

Hippocrates of Iphicrates

***

What heart can think, or tongue express,
The harm that groweth of idleness?

John Heywood

***

Every man is as lazy as he dares to be.

Ralph Waldo Emerson

***

Evil thoughts intrude in an unemployed mind, as naturally as worms are generated in a stagnant pool.

Old Latin Saying

***

Idleness is paralysis.

Roswell Dwight Hitchcock

***

50   *The Seven Deadly Sins*

Idleness travels very slowly, and poverty soon overtakes her.

John Hunter

***

Slothfulness casteth into a deep sleep; and an idle soul shall suffer hunger.

The Bible

***

Valour, gradually overpowered by the delicious poison of sloth, grows torpid.

Titus Caius Silius Italicus

***

If you are idle, be not solitary; if you are solitary, be not idle.

Samuel Johnson

***

Inactivity and deprivation of all accustomed stimulus is not rest; it is a preparation for the tomb.

Robertson Davies

***

As peace is the end of war, so to be idle is the ultimate purpose of the busy.

Samuel Johnson

***

SLOTH   51

Flee sloth; for the indolence of the soul is the decay of the body.

Cato The Elder

***

Sloth ... never arrived at the attainment of a good wish.

Cervantes

***

For a nation which has an almost evil reputation for bustle, bustle, bustle, and rush, rush, rush, we spend an enormous amount of time standing around in line in front of windows, just waiting.

Robert Benchley

***

Laziness grows on people; it begins in cobwebs, and ends in iron chains. The more business a man has to do, the more he is able to accomplish; for he learns to economize his time.

Sir Matthew Hale

***

Some people have a perfect genius for doing nothing, and doing it assiduously.

Thomas Chandler Haliburton (used pseudonym Sam Slick)

***

52   *The Seven Deadly Sins*

Trouble springs from idleness, and grievous toil from needless ease.

Benjamin Franklin

***

The idle man stands outside of God's plan, outside of the ordained scheme of things; and the truest self-respect, the noblest independence, and the most genuine dignity, are not to be found there.

Josiah Gilbert Holland (used pseudonym Timothy Titcomb)

***

There is no remedy for time misspent;
    No healing for the waste of idleness,
    Whose very languor is a punishment
    Heavier than active souls can feel or guess.

Sir Aubrey de Vere

***

The lazy man aims at nothing, and generally hits it.

James Ellis

***

The biggest sin is sitting on your ass.

Florynce Kennedy

***

SLOTH   53

Disciplined inaction.

Sir James Mackintosh

***

As sloth seldom bringeth actions to good birth; so hasty rashness always makes them abortive ere well formed.

Arthur Warwick

***

If idleness do not produce vice or malevolence, it commonly produces melancholy.

Sydney Smith

***

The ruin of most men dates from some idle moment.

George Stillman Hillard

***

Were't not affection chains thy tender days
    To the sweet glances of thy honoured love,
    I rather would entreat thy company
    To see the wonders of the world abroad
    Than, living dully sluggardized at home,
    Wear out thy youth with shapeless idleness.

William Shakespeare

***

The Seven Deadly Sins

Is there anything so wretched as to look at a man of fine abilities doing nothing?

Edwin Hubbell Chapin

***

As idle as a painted ship
   Upon a painted ocean.

Samuel Taylor Coleridge

***

Idleness is both a great sin, and the cause of many more.

Bishop Robert South

***

That destructive siren, sloth, is ever to be avoided.

Horace

***

Sloth is the torpidity of the mental faculties; the sluggard is a living insensible.

Johann Georg von Zimmermann

***

Idleness is the holiday of fools.

Philip Dormer Stanhope, 4th Earl of Chesterfield,

***

SLOTH   55

But how can he expect that others should
　　Build for him, sow for him, and at his call
　　Love him, who for himself will take no heed at all?

William Wordsworth

***

Their only labour was to kill the time;
　　And labour dire it is, and weary woe,
　　They sit, they loll, turn o'er some idle rhyme,
　　Then, rising sudden, to the glass they go,
　　Or saunter forth, with tottering steps and slow.

James Thomson

***

Indolence is the sleep of the mind.

Luc de Clapier de Vauvanargues

***

Rather do what is nothing to the purpose than be idle; that the devil may find thee doing. The bird that sits is easily shot, when fliers scape the fowler. Idleness is the Dead Sea that swallows all the virtues, and the self-made sepulchre of a living man.

Francis Quarles

***

Laziness may appear attractive, but work gives satisfaction.

Anne Frank

***

Humanity is constitutionally lazy.

Josiah Gilbert Holland (used pseudonym Timothy Titcomb)

***

If you are idle, you are on the road to ruin; and there are few stopping-places upon it. It is rather a precipice than a road.

Henry Ward Beecher

***

Many are idly busy. Domitian was busy, but then it was catching flies.

Jeremy Taylor

***

The bees can abide no drones amongst them; but as soon as they begin to be idle, they kill them.

Plato

***

Idleness is many, gathered miseries in one name.

Jean Paul Friedrich Richter

***

I pity the man overwhelmed with the weight of his own leisure.

Voltaire

***

An idler is a watch that wants both hands;
As useless if it goes as when it stands.

William Cowper

***

Idleness is the stupidity of the body; and stupidity the idleness of the mind.

Johann Gottfried Seume

***

We excuse our sloth under the pretext of difficulty.

Quintilian

***

Nine-tenths of the miseries and vices of mankind proceed from idleness.

Thomas Carlyle

***

Stagnant satisfaction!

Samuel Smiles

***

58   *The Seven Deadly Sins*

Thee too, my Paridel! she mark'd thee there,
  Stretch'd on the rack of a too easy chair,
  And heard thy everlasting yarn confess
  The Pains and Penalties of Idleness.

Alexander Pope

***

Slovenliness is a lazy and beastly negligence of a man's own person, whereby he becomes so sordid as to be offensive to those about him.

Theophrastus

***

Busy idleness urges us on.

Horace

***

Every hour of lost time is a chance of future misfortune.

Napoleon Bonaparte

***

Enjoyment stops where indolence begins.

Robert Pollok

***

SLOTH   59

A man who has no office to go to - I don't care who he is - is a trial of which you can have no conception.

George Bernard Shaw

***

Laziness is a good deal like money - the more a man has of it, the more he seems to want.

Henry Wheeler Shaw (used pseudonyms Josh Billings and Uncle Esek)

***

How various his employments whom the world
    Calls idle; and who justly in return
    Esteems that busy world an idler too!

William Cowper

***

'Tis the voice of the sluggard; I heard him complain,
    "You have waked me too soon, I must slumber again."
    As the door on its hinges, so he on his bed,
    Turns his sides and his shoulders and his heavy head.
    "A little more sleep, and a little more slumber;"
    Thus he wastes half his days, and his hours without number,
    And when he gets up, he sits folding his hands,
    Or walks about sauntering, or trifling he stands.

Isaac Watts

***

The Seven Deadly Sins

Too much idleness, I have observed, fills up a man's time more completely and leaves him less his own master, than any sort of employment whatsoever.

Edmund Burke

***

Idleness is an inlet to disorder, and makes way for licentiousness. People that have nothing to do are quickly tired of their own company.

Jeremy Collier

***

A lazy person, whatever the talents with which he starts out, has condemned himself to second-rate thoughts, and to second-rate friends.

Cyril Connolly

***

Men will lie on their backs, talking about the fall of man, and never make an effort to get up.

Henry David Thoreau

***

Even if a farmer intends to loaf, he gets up in time to have an early start.

Edgar Watson Howe

***

If you wish at once to do nothing and be respectable nowadays, the best pretext is to be at work on some profound study.

Sir Leslie Stephen

***

Inactivity is death.

Benito Mussolini

***

The gloomy and the resentful are always found among those who have nothing to do or who do nothing

Samuel Johnson

***

I have also seen the world, and after long experience have discovered that ennui is our greatest enemy, and remunerative labour our most lasting friend.

Justus Moser

***

Indifference, to me, is the epitome of evil.

Elie Wiesel

***

62   *The Seven Deadly Sins*

The world is a dangerous place to live, not because of the people who are evil, but because of the people who don't do anything about it.

Albert Einstein

***

It is not only what we do, but also what we do not do, for which we are accountable.

Moliere

***

Throughout history it has been the inaction of those who could have acted, the indifference of those who should have known better, the silence of the voice of justice when it mattered most, that has made it possible for evil to triumph.

Haile Selassie

***

GREED
(Latin, *avaritia*)

The love of money is the root of all evil.

The Bible

The Delphic Oracle, in its two most important messages to the ancient Greeks, had enjoined 'know thyself' and 'nothing to excess'. And greed, like its close cousins, gluttony and lust, is unquestionably a sin of excess. In the eyes of the medieval church, it applied, in particular, to the accumulation of wealth. Greed was considered a form of idolatry, connected in the book of Exodus with the worship of the golden calf, the greedy person prizing money and possessions more highly than God.

The transition from a pre-modern religious era to a modern, secular age is best characterised by the replacement of spiritual with material values. Our preoccupation with the gaining of possessions in the here and now rather than the pursuit of rewards in the world to come has, in these highly acquisitive times, encouraged everywhere the spread of greed and avarice.

Moreover, the environmental impact of our rapaciousness cannot be overstated. Rowan Williams, Archbishop of Canterbury, recently said that man's destruction of the planet was fuelled by greed, selfishness and stupidity. The poorest and most vulnerable, and our children and grandchildren would pay the heaviest price for climate change, he added.

We are all, of course, currently enduring the economic consequences of the unbridled greed and cupidity of the banking fraternity: to paraphrase Winston Churchill, never has so much harm been done to so many by so few!

>>>

GREED 65

Rich men without convictions are more dangerous in modern society than poor women without chastity.

George Bernard Shaw

***

A captive fettered at the oar of gain.

William Falconer

***

Avarice starves its possessor to fatten those who come after, and who are eagerly awaiting the demise of the accumulator.

Sir Fulke Greville, 1st Baron Brooke, Lord Brooke

***

The avarice of mankind is insatiable.

Aristotle

***

Wealth in the gross is death, but life diffus'd,
  As poison heals, in just proportion us'd.

Alexander Pope

***

Why Mammon sits before a million hearths
  Where God is bolted out from every house.

Philip James Bailey

***

66 The *Seven Deadly Sins*

Parsimony is enough to make the master of the golden mines as poor as he that has nothing; for a man may be brought to a morsel of bread by parsimony as well as profusion.

Henry Home, Lord Kames

***

All good things of this world are no further good to us than as they are of use; and whatever we may heap up to give to others, we enjoy only as much as we can use, and no more.

Daniel Defoe

***

He who is always in a hurry to be wealthy and immersed in the study of augmenting his fortune has lost the arms of reason and deserted the post of virtue.

Horace

***

Avarice, the spur of industry.

David Hume

***

Avarice is the vice of declining years.

George Bancroft

***

GREED   67

Avarice is to the intellect what sensuality is to the morals.

Mrs. Anna Brownell Jameson

***

This avarice
  Sticks deeper, grows with more pernicious root
  Than summer-seeming lust, and it hath been
  The sword of our slain kings.

William Shakespeare

***

The darkest day in a man's career is that wherein he fancies there is some easier way of getting a dollar than by squarely earning it.

Horace Greeley

***

It is nor for the sake of life that some men make fortunes; for, blinded by avarice, they live only for the sake of making fortunes.

Juvenal

***

The covetous man pines in plenty, like Tantalus up to the chin in water, and yet thirsty.

Thomas Adams

***

68   The *Seven Deadly Sins*

There are two considerations which always embitter the heart of an avaricious man - the one is a perpetual thirst after more riches, the other the prospect of leaving what he has already acquired.

Henry Fielding

***

Some men are called sagacious, merely on account of their avarice; whereas a child can clench its fist the moment it is born.

William Shenstone

***

The avaricious man is kind to no person, but he is most unkind to himself.

John Kyrle

***

Avarice in old age is foolish; for what can be more absurd than to increase our provisions for the road, the nearer we approach to our journey's end?

Cicero

***

To be thankful for what we grasp exceeding our proportion is to add hypocrisy to injustice.

Charles Lamb

***

It is one of the worst effects of prosperity to make a man a vortex instead of a fountain; so that, instead of throwing out, he learns only to draw in.

Henry Ward Beecher

***

Riches, like insects, when conceal'd they lie,
Wait but for wings, and in their season fly.
Who sees pale Mammon pine amidst his store,
Sees but a backward steward for the poor;
This year a reservoir, to keep and spare;
The next a fountain, spouting thro' his heir
In lavish streams to quench a country's thirst,
And men and dogs shall drink him till they burst.

Alexander Pope

***

I am a Millionaire. That is my religion.

George Bernard Shaw

***

70   The *Seven Deadly Sins*

In plain truth, it is not want, but rather abundance, that creates avarice.

Michel Eyquem de Montaigne

***

When all the sins are old in us,
    And go upon crutches, covetousness
    Does but lie in her cradle.

Thomas Dekker

***

It is by bribing, not so often by being bribed, that wicked politicians bring ruin on mankind. Avarice is a rival to the pursuits of many.

Edmund Burke

***

So for a good old-gentlemanly vice,
    I think I must take up with avarice.

Lord Byron

***

It may be remarked for the comfort of honest poverty that avarice reigns most in those who have but few good qualities to recommend them. This is a weed that will grow in a barren soil.

Thomas Hughes

***

GREED 71

And in his lap a masse of coyne he told
    And turned upside down, to feede his eye
    And covetous desire with his huge treasury.

Edmund Spenser

***

Some o'erenamor'd of their bags run mad,
    Groan under gold, yet weep for want of bread.

Edward Young

***

Extreme avarice is nearly always mistaken; there is no passion
which is oftener further away from
its mark, nor upon which the present has so much power to the
prejudice of the future.

Francois Duc de la Rochefoucauld

***

O cursed lust of gold; when for thy sake The fool throws up his
    interest in both worlds,
    First starved in this, then damn'd in that to come.

Hugh Blair

***

Capitalism is founded on greed and envy.

Charles Long

***

The lust of avarice has so totally seized upon mankind that their wealth seems rather to possess them than they possess their wealth.

Pliny the Elder

***

With this there grows
    In my most ill-compos'd affection such
    A stanchless avarice that, were I King,
    I should cut off the nobles for their lands,
    Desire his jewels, and this other's house,
    And my more-having would be as a sauce
    To make me hunger more, that I should forge
    Quarrels unjust against the good and loyal,
    Destroying them for wealth.

William Shakespeare

***

Poverty is in want of much, but avarice of everything.

Syrus

***

Avarice is generally the last passion of those lives of which the first part has been squandered in pleasure, and the second devoted to ambition.

Samuel Johnson

***

He sat amid his bags, and, with a look
  Which hell might be ashamed of, drove the poor
  Away unalmsed; and midst abundance died -
  Sorest of evils! - died of utter want.

Robert Pollok

***

The love of money increases to the extent that money itself increases.

Juvenal

***

Why are we so blind? That which we improve, we have, that which we hoard is not for ourselves.

Dorothee DeLuzy

***

Covetous men are fools, miserable wretches, buzzards, madmen who live by themselves, in perpetual slavery, fear, suspicion, sorrow, discontent, with more of gall than honey in their enjoyments; who are rather possessed by their money than possessors of it.

Robert Burton

***

74   The *Seven Deadly Sins*

The love of gold that meanest rage,
    And latest folly of man's sinking age,
    Which, rarely venturing in the van of life,
    While nobler passions wage their heated strife,
    Comes skulking last with selfishness and fear
    And dies collecting lumber in the rear!

Thomas Moore

***

Study rather to fill your mind than your coffers; knowing that gold and silver were originally mingled with dirt, until avarice or ambition parted them.

Seneca

***

People who are hard, grasping and always ready to take advantage of their neighbours become very rich.

George Bernard Shaw

***

To me avarice seems not so much a vice as a deplorable piece of madness.

Sir Thomas Browne

***

The objects of avarice and ambition differ only in their greatness. A miser is as furious about a halfpenny as the man of ambition about the conquest of a kingdom.

Adam Smith

***

Avarice often produces opposite effects; there is an infinite number of people who sacrifice all their property to doubtful and distant expectations; others despise great future advantages to obtain present interests of a trifling nature.

Francois Duc de la Rochefoucauld

***

A poor spirit is poorer than a poor purse. A very few pounds a year would ease a man of the scandal of avarice.

Jonathan Swift

***

The man who worships mere wealth is a snob.

Anthony Trollope

***

Greed is all right . . . Greed is healthy. You can be greedy and still feel good about yourself.

Ivan F. Boesky

***

76   The *Seven Deadly Sins*

The avaricious man is like the barren, sandy ground of the desert, which sucks in all the rain and dews with greediness, but yields no fruitful herbs or plants for the benefit of others.

Zeno

***

Many have been ruined by their fortunes; many have escaped ruin by the want of fortune. To obtain it, the great have become little, and the little great.

Johann Georg von Zimmermann

***

The covetous man is like a camel with a great hunch on his back; heaven's gate must be made higher and broader, or he will hardly get in.

Thomas Adams

***

If money be not thy servant, it will be thy master. The covetous man cannot so properly be said to possess wealth, as that it may be said to possess him.

Francis Bacon

***

Covetousness is a sort of mental gluttony, not confined to money, but craving honour, and feeding on selfishness.

Sebastien-Roch-Nicolas de Chamfort

***

GREED   77

When all sins are old in us, and go upon crutches, covetousness does but then lie in her cradle.

Thomas Dekker

***

The prodigality of millionaires is comparable only to their greed of gain. Let some whim or passion seize them and money is of no account. In fact these Croesuses find whims and passions harder to come by than gold.

Honore de Balzac

***

To do all the talking and not be willing to listen is a form of greed.

Democritus

***

Kill no more pigeons than you can eat.

Benjamin Franklin

***

Do not hold grain waiting for higher prices when people are hungry.

Zoroaster

***

78   The *Seven Deadly Sins*

The lust of avarice as so totally seized upon mankind that their wealth seems rather to possess them than they possess their wealth.

Pliny the Elder

***

Avarice is the vice of declining years.

George Bancroft

***

For at least another hundred years we must pretend to ourselves and to every one that fair is foul and foul is fair; for foul is useful and fair is not. Avarice and usury and precaution must be our gods for a little longer still.

John Maynard Keynes

***

Prudery is a kind of avarice, the worst of all.

Stendhal

***

Ennui has made more gamblers than avarice, more drunkards than thirst, and perhaps as many suicides as despair.

Buddha

***

GREED 79

Love is always a stranger in the house of avarice.

Andreas Capellanus

***

Enriched beyond the dreams of any normal person's avarice, she accumulated possessions with a single-minded lust that calls to mind those ancient Romans who gorged themselves, then vomited so they could gorge again.

Russell Watson

***

Avarice has ruined more men than prodigality, and the blindest thoughtlessness of expenditure has not destroyed so many fortunes as the calculating but insatiable lust of accumulation.

Charles Caleb Colton

***

All social rules and all relations between individuals are eroded by a cash economy, avarice drags Pluto himself out of the bowels of the earth.

Karl Marx

***

Another good thing about being poor is that when you are seventy your children will not have declared you legally insane in order to gain control of your estate.

Woody Allen

***

80   The *Seven Deadly Sins*

We tend to forget that happiness doesn't come as a result of getting something we don't have, but rather of recognizing and appreciating what we do have.

Frederick Koenig

***

The dynamo of our economic system is self-interest which may range from mere petty greed to admirable types of self-expression.

Felix Frankfurter

***

New York City is a great monument to the power of money and greed.

Frank Lloyd Wright

***

If we go on the way we have, the fault is our greed [and] if we are not willing [to change], we will disappear from the face of the globe, to be replaced by the insect.

Jacques Cousteau

WRATH
(Latin, *ira*)

People who fly into a rage always make a bad landing.

Will Rogers

Wrath can be defined as uncontrolled feelings of anger, rage and even hatred, often revealing itself in the wish to seek vengeance, even, in extreme cases, outside the boundaries of the conventional justice system. Virtually all peacetime political violence, of which urban terrorism is the most pernicious example, are born of feelings of grievance for past wrongs manifesting themselves as anger.

There is no doubt that Adolf Hitler felt genuine anger when he reflected upon the punitive terms of the Versailles Treaty or the imagined 'crimes' of the Jewish people against the Germanic 'race'. Dante characterised wrath as 'love of justice perverted to revenge and spite'.

Originally the sin of wrath also embraced anger directed inwardly rather than outwardly. Suicide was therefore seen as the ultimate expression of anger directed internally, a sacrilegious rejection of God's greatest gift - of life. This explains why the Church focused so much on suicide - and to such an extent that its perpetrators were, until quite recent times, generally denied burial in consecrated ground.

The timeless theme of rage leading to vengeance is expressed with some sympathy and explanation by the Greek tragic playwrights, most notably in Euripides' *Medea*. Even though she commits the most unspeakable crime of infanticide, as a desperate means of getting back at the 'husband' who had abandoned her, the dramatist appears to be saying that, if you oppress an already downtrodden individual or group and treat them with contempt for long enough, their anger, when it eventually erupts, will be beyond reason and justification and, though it cannot be condoned, is somehow understandable.

>>>

The pain is in my head; 'tis is in my heart;
  Tis everywhere; it rages like a madness,
  And I most wonder how my reason holds.

Thomas Otway

***

Anger is one letter short of danger.

Anon

***

They could neither of them speak for rage, and so fell a-sputtering at one another like two roasting apples.

William Congreve

***

Anger makes dull men witty, but it keeps them poor.

Francis Bacon

***

Rage is a short-lived fury.

Jean-Antoine Petit-Senn

***

84 The *Seven Deadly Sins*

When one is transported by rage, it is best to observe attentively the effects on those who deliver themselves over to the same passion.

Plutarch

***

Oppose not rage while rage is in its force, but give it way awhile and let it waste.

William Shakespeare

***

Get mad, then get over it.

Colin Powell

***

Hasty wrath and heedless hazardy do breed repentance late and lasting infamy.

Edmund Spenser

***

If a small thing has the power to make you angry, does that not indicate something about your size?

Sydney J. Harris

***

WRATH   85

There is nothing more galling to angry people than the coolness of those on whom they wish to vent their spleen.

Alexandre Dumas

***

In the beginning the Universe was created. This has made a lot of people very angry and been widely regarded as a bad move.

Douglas Adams

***

He who angers you conquers you.

Elizabeth Kenny

***

For every minute you are angry, you lose sixty seconds of happiness.

Anon.

***

Anger ventilated often hurries toward forgiveness; and concealed often hardens into revenge.

Edward G. Bulwer-Lytton

***

Never write a letter while you are angry.

Chinese Proverb

***

86   The *Seven Deadly Sins*

Mud, raised by hurricanes, wells up in the noblest and purest of hearts.

Honore de Balzac

***

The world needs *anger*. The world often continues to allow evil because it isn't angry enough.

Bede Jarrett

***

Never go to bed mad. Stay up and fight.

Phyllis Diller

***

'T was grief no more, or grief and rage were one within her soul; at last 't was rage alone.

John Dryden

***

In certain trying circumstances, urgent circumstances, desperate circumstances, profanity furnishes a relief denied even to prayer.

Mark Twain

***

Expressing anger is a form of public littering.

Willard Gaylin

***

Resentment is like taking poison and waiting for the other person to die.

Malachy McCourt

***

Anger as soon as fed is dead -
   'Tis starving makes it fat.

Emily Dickinson

***

If you kick a stone in anger, you'll hurt your own foot.

Korean Proverb

***

Anger dwells only in the bosom of fools.

Albert Einstein

***

88   The *Seven Deadly Sins*

No man can think clearly when his fists are clenched.

George Jean Nathan

***

An angry man who suppresses his passions thinks worse than he speaks; and an angry man that will chide speaks worse than he thinks.

Francis Bacon

***

Anger is short-lived madness.

Horace

***

For pale and trembling anger rushes in
    With faltering speech, and eyes that wildly stare,
    Fierce as the tiger, madder than the seas,
    Desperate and armed with more than human strength.

John Armstrong

***

Anger and jealousy can no more bear to lose sight of their objects than love.

George Eliot

***

WRATH   89

To abandon yourself to rage is often to bring upon yourself the fault of another.

Pope Agapet

***

Rage is the shortest passion of our souls,
    Like narrow brooks that rise with sudden showers,
    It swells in haste, and falls again as soon.
    Still as it ebbs, the softer thoughts flow in,
    And the deceiver, love, supplies its place.

Nicholas Rowe

***

If you're angry at a loved one, hug that person. And mean it. You may not want to hug - which is all the more reason to do so. It's hard to stay angry when someone shows they love you, and that's precisely what happens when we hug each other.

Walter Anderson

***

Do not teach your children never to be angry; teach them *how* to be angry.

Lyman Abbott

***

Anger blows out the lamp of the mind.

Robert G. Ingersoll

***

90   The *Seven Deadly Sins*

Sometimes when I'm angry I have the right to be angry, but that doesn't give me the right to be cruel.

Anon.

***

Next time you're mad, try dancing out your anger.

Sweetpea Tyler

***

A man that does not know how to be angry does not know how to be good.

Henry Ward Beecher

***

Her colour changed, her face was not the same,
   And hollow groans from her deep spirit came;
   Her hair stood up; convulsive rage possess'd
   Her trembling limbs, and heaved her lab'ring breast.

John Dryden

***

Always write angry letters to your enemies. Never mail them.

James Fallows

***

WRATH 91

Anger is never without a reason, but seldom with a good one.

Benjamin Franklin

***

It takes two flints to make a fire.

Louisa May Alcott

***

Not the fastest horse can catch a word spoken in anger.

Chinese Proverb

***

Temper tantrums, however fun they may be to throw, rarely solve whatever problem is causing them.

Lemony Snicket

***

I don't have to attend every argument I'm invited to.

Anon.

***

Can anger survive without his hypocrisy?

Jareb Teague

***

92   The *Seven Deadly Sins*

Holding on to anger is like grasping a hot coal with the intent of throwing it at someone else; you are the one who gets burned.

Buddha

***

Anger and folly walk cheek by jowl.

Benjamin Franklin

***

Rage is mental imbecility.

Hosea Ballou

***

Malice drinks one-half of its own poison.

Seneca

***

Anger is a killing thing: it kills the man who angers, for each rage leaves him less than he had been before - it takes something from him.

Louis L'Armour

***

Never strike your wife - even with a flower.

Hindu Proverb

***

WRATH 93

Speak when you are angry and you will make the best speech you will ever regret.

Ambrose Bierce

***

When angry, count four; when very angry, swear.

Mark Twain

***

Anger is a bad counsellor.

French Proverb

***

Resentment is an extremely bitter diet, and eventually poisonous. I have no desire to make my own toxins.

Neil Kinnock

***

To carry a grudge is like being stung to death by one bee.

William H. Walton

***

The best remedy for a short temper is a long walk.

Jacqueline Schiff

***

94   The *Seven Deadly Sins*

When a man sends you an impudent letter, sit right down and give it back to him with interest ten times compounded, and then throw both letters in the wastebasket.

Elbert Hubbard

***

No man can think clearly when his fists are clenched.

George Jean Nathan

***

Consider how much more you often suffer from your anger and grief, than from those very things for which you are angry and grieved.

Marcus Antonius

***

A man is about as big as the things that make him angry.

Winston Churchill

***

For every minute you are angry you lose sixty seconds of happiness.

Ralph Waldo Emerson

***

WRATH   95

Men often make up in wrath what they want in reason.

William R. Alger

***

The angry people are those people who are most afraid.

Robert Anthony

***

Whatever is begun in anger ends in shame.

Benjamin Franklin

***

If you are patient in one moment of anger, you will escape a hundred days of sorrow.

Chinese Proverb

***

I know of no more disagreeable sensation than to be left feeling generally angry without anybody in particular to be angry at.

Frank Moore Colby

***

When you are offended at any man's fault, turn to yourself and study your own failings. Then you will forget your anger.

Epictetus

***

96 The *Seven Deadly Sins*

Let us not look back in anger, nor forward in fear, but around in awareness.

James Thurber

***

So long as a man is angry he cannot be in the right.

Chinese Proverb

***

Eat a third and drink a third and leave the remaining third of your stomach empty. Then, when you get angry, there will be sufficient room for your rage.

Babylonian Talmud

***

Man should forget his anger before he lies down to sleep.

Gandhi

***

ENVY
(Latin, *invidia*)

Envy consists in seeing things never in themselves, but only in their relations. If you desire glory, you may envy Napoleon, but Napoleon envied Caesar, Caesar envied Alexander, and Alexander, I dare say, envied Hercules, who never existed.

Bertrand Russell

Envy could be described as an often unquenchable desire to possess something that another has which they believe they lack themselves. As such, it is one of the most potent sources of unhappiness. It differs from greed which is concerned principally with the acquisition of material possessions, whilst envy may have a more general application, for example, resentment at another's success, status, love or happiness.

Dante defined envy as "love of one's own good perverted to a desire to deprive other men of theirs." Dante's concept is thus similar to the German term 'schadenfreude' which refers to the joy we may derive from the misfortune of others.

It is a regrettable but undeniable aspect of human psychology that the level of contentment of an individual is often measured against the perceived happiness or success of others. Interestingly, the definition of 'poverty' in most modern societies is couched in relative terms, that is, based on a comparison with the economic position of others – the mean

98   The *Seven Deadly Sins*

standard of living in that country – rather than on factors more closely associated with deprivation in absolute terms.

Sexual jealousy – surely one of the strongest emotions suffered by human beings - has, throughout the ages, led to crimes of passion that seem utterly irrational and out keeping with the character of the perpetrator. Envy can thus be said to lead to a loss of control and to the kinds of anti-social behaviour that all societies must guard themselves against.

>>>

ENVY 99

Men of noble birth are noted to be envious towards new men when they rise; for the distance is all told, and it is like a deceit of the eye, that when others come on they think themselves going back.

Francis Bacon

***

Envy is the art of counting the other fellow's blessings instead of your own.

Harold Coffin

***

Envy: I am Envy, begotten of a Chimney-sweeper, and
an Oyster-wife: I cannot read, and therefore wish all books
burn'd. I am leane with seeing others eate: O that there
would come a famine o'er all the world, that all might die,
and I live alone, then thou should'st see how fat I'de be. But
must thou sit, and I stand? Come downe with a vengeance.

Christopher Marlowe

***

I envy people who can just look at a sunset. I wonder how you can shoot it. There is nothing more grotesque to me than a vacation.

Dustin Hoffman

***

100   The *Seven Deadly Sins*

The envious will die, but envy never.

Moliere

***

A sound heart is the life of the flesh: but envy the rottenness of the bones.

Bible, Proverbs

***

Envy is like a fly that passes all the body's sounder parts, and dwells upon the sores.

Arthur Chapman

***

On the one hand, people think they own kids; they feel that they have the right to tell the kids what to do. On the other hand, people envy kids. We'd like to be kids our whole lives. Kids get to do what they do. They live on their instincts.

David Duchovny

***

Men know they are sexual exiles. They wander the earth seeking satisfaction, craving and despising, never content. There is nothing in that anguished motion for women to envy.

Camille Paglia

***

ENVY 101

Never underestimate the power of jealousy and the power of envy to destroy. Never underestimate that.

Oliver Stone

***

It is the practice of the multitude to bark at eminent men, as little dogs do at strangers.

Seneca

***

How bitter a thing it is to look into happiness through another man's eyes!

William Shakespeare

***

As a moth gnaws a garment, so doth envy consume a man.

St. John Chrysostom

***

Nothing can allay the rage of biting envy.

Claudian (Claudianus)

***

Envy lurks at the bottom of the human heart, like a viper in its hole.

Honore de Balzac

***

102   The *Seven Deadly Sins*

Envy lies between two beings equal in nature though unequal in circumstances.

Jeremy Collier

***

Many men profess to hate another, but no man owns envy, as being an enmity or displeasure for no cause but goodness or felicity.

Jeremy Taylor

***

As rust corrupts iron, so envy corrupts man.

Antisthenes

***

It was well said that envy keeps no holidays.

Francis Bacon

***

To our betters we can reconcile ourselves, if you please - respecting them sincerely, laughing at their jokes, making allowance for their stupidities, meekly suffering their insolence; but we can't pardon our equals going beyond us.

William Makepeace Thackeray

***

ENVY   103

There is some good in public envy, whereas in private there is none; for public envy is as an ostracism that eclipseth men when they grow too great; and therefore it is a bridle also to great ones to keep within bounds.

Francis Bacon

***

Not on thy sole, but on thy soul, harsh Jew,
    Thou mak'st thy knife keen; but no metal can--
    No, not the hangman's axe - bear half the keenness
    Of thy sharp envy.

William Shakespeare

***

I don't believe that there is a human creature in his senses, arrived to maturity, that at some time or other has not been carried away by this passion (sc. envy) in good earnest; yet I never met with any one who dared own he was guilty of it but in jest.

Bernard Mandeville

***

For something in the envy of the small
    Still loves the vast democracy of death!
        Lord Edward Robert Bulwer- Lytton, 1st Earl of Lytton

***

104   The *Seven Deadly Sins*

Save those who fill the highest stations, I know of none more unfortunate than those who envy them.

Mme. Francoise d'Aubigne de Maintenon

***

Envy, like the worm, never runs but to the fairest fruit; like a cunning bloodhound, it singles out the fattest deer in the flock. Abraham's riches were the Philistines' envy; and Jacob's blessing bred Esau's hatred.

J. Beaumont

***

To be an object of hatred and aversion to their contemporaries has been the usual fate of all those whose merit has raised them above the common level. The man who submits to the shafts of envy for the sake of noble objects pursues a judicious course for his own lasting fame. Hatred dies with its object, while merit soon breaks forth in full splendour, and his glory is handed down to posterity in never-dying strains.

Thucydides

***

Envy, if surrounded on all sides by the brightness of another's prosperity, like the scorpion confined within a circle of fire, will sting itself to death.

Charles Caleb Colton

***

ENVY 105

I have never been given to envy - save for the envy I feel toward those people who have the ability to make a marriage work and endure happily.

Paul Getty

***

The hen of our neighbour appears to us a goose, says the Oriental proverb.

Dorothee DeLuzy

***

When I think over what I have said, I envy dumb people.

Seneca

***

In Britain, because I live here, I can also run into problems of envy and competition. But all this is just in a day's work for a writer. You can't put stuff out there without someone calling you a complete fool. Oh, well.

Alain de Botton

***

Such men as he be never at heart's ease
    Whiles they behold a greater than themselves,
    And therefore are they very dangerous.

William Shakespeare

***

But, oh! what mighty magician can assuage
 A woman's envy?

George Granville, Lord Landsdowne

***

Just so far as we are pleased at finding faults, are we displeased at finding perfection.

Johann Kaspar Lavater (John Caspar Lavater)

***

Envy, like fire, soars upwards.

Tacitus

***

They say that love and tears are learned without any master; and I may say that there is no great need of studying at the court to learn envy and revenge.

Nicolas Caussin

***

Base envy withers at another's joy,
 And hates that excellence it cannot reach.

James Thomson

***

ENVY   107

Envy is the deformed and distorted offspring of egotism; and when we reflect on the strange and disproportioned character of the parent, we cannot wonder at the perversity and waywardness of the child.

William Hazlitt

***

That incessant envy wherewith the common rate of mankind pursues all superior natures to their own.

Jonathan Swift

***

To all apparent beauties blind,
Each blemish strikes an envious mind.

John Gay

***

When we envy another, we make their virtue our vice.

Nicolas Boileau-Despreaux

***

'Tis the beginning of hell in this life, and a passion not to be excused. Every other sin hath some pleasure annexed to it, or will admit of an excuse: envy alone wants both.

Robert Burton

***

Better it is to be envied than pitied.

Herodotus

***

Envy, like a cold prison, benumbs and stupefies; and, conscious of its own impotence, folds its arms in despair.

Jeremy Collier

***

The envious pine at others' success; no greater punishment than envy was devised by Sicilian tyrants.

Horace

***

Whoever envies another confesses his superiority.

Samuel Johnson

***

Envy is the daughter of pride, the author of murder and revenge, the beginner of secret sedition and the perpetual tormentor of virtue. Envy is the filthy slime of the soul; a venom, a poison, or quicksilver which consumeth the flesh and drieth up the marrow of the bones.

Socrates

***

ENVY 109

And next to him malicious Envy rode
    Upon a ravenous wolfe, and still did chaw
    Between his cankered teeth a venomous tode,
    That all the poison ran about his jaw;
    But inwardly he chawed his own maw
    At neighbour's wealth that made him ever sad
    For death it was when any good he saw;
    And wept, that cause of weeping none he had;
    And when he heard of harme he waxed wondrous glad.

Edmund Spenser

***

When any person of really eminent virtue becomes the object of envy, the clamour and abuse by which he is assailed is but the sign and accompaniment of his success in doing service to the public. And if he is a truly wise man, he will take no more notice of it than the moon does of the howling of the dogs. Her only answer to them is to shine on.

Archbishop Richard Whately

***

Envy will merit as its shade pursue,
    But like a shadow, proves the substance true.

Alexander Pope

***

110   The *Seven Deadly Sins*

Envy assails the noblest: the winds howl around the highest peaks.

Ovid

***

Envy, like flame, blackens that which is above it, and which it cannot reach.

Jean-Antoine Petit-Senn

***

Envy, the attendant of the empty mind.

Pindar

***

We spend our time envying people whom we wouldn't wish to be.

Jean Rostand

***

Stones and sticks are thrown only at fruit-bearing trees.

Moslih Eddin

***

If we did but know how little some enjoy of the great things that they possess, there would not be much envy in the world.

Edward Young

***

ENVY 111

Arise, fair sun, and kill the envious moon,
    Who is already sick and pale with grief
    That thou her maid art far more fair than she.
    Be not her maid, since she is envious.
    Her vestal livery is but sick and green,
    And none but fools do wear it. Cast it off.

William Shakespeare

***

Keep yourselves far from envy; it eateth up and taketh away good actions, like as fire eateth up and burneth wood.

Muhammad

***

I envy paranoids; they actually feel people are paying attention to them.

Susan Sontag

***

Nothing sharpens sight like envy.

Thomas Fuller

***

Our envy of others devours us most of all.

Alexander Solzhenitsyn

***

112   The *Seven Deadly Sins*

Envy, among other ingredients, has a mixture of the love of justice in it. We are more angry at undeserved than at deserved good fortune.

William Hazlitt

***

Mediocrity doesn't mean average intelligence; it means an average intelligence that resents and envies its betters.

Ayn Rand

***

Envy comes from people's ignorance of, or lack of belief in, their own gifts.

Jean Vanier

***

Love looks through a telescope; envy, through a microscope.

Josh Billings

***

If I am fool, it is, at least, a doubting one; and I envy no one the certainty of his self-approved wisdom.

Lord Byron

***

ENVY   113

Envy is of all others the most ungratifying and disconsolate passion. There is power for ambition, pleasure for luxury, and pelf even for covetousness; but envy gets no reward but vexation.

Jeremy Collier

***

I doubt that we Americans can come to terms with our money neuroses without understanding the more florid pathology of the very rich for it is our envy and admiration of the rich that supports their habit and keeps us hooked ourselves.

Philip Slater

***

Communism possesses a language which every people can understand - its elements are hunger, envy, and death.

Heinrich Heine

***

Moral indignation in most cases is, 2% moral, 48% indignation, and 50% envy.

Vittorio De Sica

***

Envy is an insult to oneself.

Yevgeny Yevtushenko

***

114   The *Seven Deadly Sins*

Our envy always lasts longer than the happiness of those we envy.

Heraclitus

***

Jealousy is both reasonable and belongs to reasonable men, while envy is base and belongs to the base, for the one makes himself get good things by jealousy, while the other does not allow his neighbour to have them through envy.

Aristotle

***

Envy, to which th' ignoble mind's a slave,
    Is emulation in the learn'd or brave.

Alexander Pope

***

Nearly every glamorous, wealthy, successful career woman you might envy now started out as some kind of schlep.

Helen Gurley Brown

***

PRIDE
(Latin, *superbia*)

It seems that nature, which has so wisely disposed our bodily organs with a view to our happiness, has also bestowed on us pride, to spare us the pain of being aware of our imperfections.
Francois Duc de la Rochefoucauld

Pride (or *hubris* or vanity) is traditionally viewed as the original and most serious of the deadly sins and, indeed, the fountainhead of most, if not all of the others. It is a blend of arrogance and self-adoration, a form of idol-worship which places oneself rather than God at the centre of one's universe. No wonder then that the medieval mind took such a dim view of it. Dante's definition of pride was 'love of self perverted to hatred and contempt for one's neighbour'. In the medieval Christian tale it was Pride that caused Lucifer's Fall from heaven.

When we think of all the wars caused, throughout human history, by vanity, we see everywhere the fear of loss of face and, in modern times especially, the refusal to come to the negotiating table with one's enemies, surely the **first** people we should talk to (the IRA, PLO, Hamas, the Taliban etc).

In Homer's *Iliad*, when Agamemnon launched the decade-long Trojan war, which would destroy tens of thousands of lives, it was to heal the damaged pride of his brother Menelaus, whose wife, Helen, had run off with (or been abducted by) Paris, the Trojan prince. In Greek tragedy, *hubris* is commonly answered by *nemesis*, and Agamemnon, who also sacrificed his own daughter, Iphigenia, so that the Greek fleet could sail (otherwise he would have lost face before the Greek host), was duly slain by his wife Clytemnestra on his return to Mycenae from Troy.

PRIDE   117

A man's own vanity is a swindler that never lacks for a dupe.

Honore de Balzac

***

Pride is a powerful narcotic, but it doesn't do much for the auto-immune system.

Stuart Stevens

***

Nobody can be so amusingly arrogant as a young man who has just discovered an old idea and thinks it is his own.

Sydney J. Harris

***

Wounded vanity knows when it is mortally hurt; and limps off the field, piteous, all disguises thrown away. But pride carries its banner to the last; and fast as it is driven from one field unfurls it in another, never admitting that there is a shade less honour in the second field than in the first, or in the third than in the second.

Helen Hunt Jackson

***

Pride requires very costly food - its keeper's happiness.

Charles Caleb Colton

***

118   The *Seven Deadly Sins*

The charity that hastens to proclaim its good deeds, ceases to be charity, and is only pride and ostentation.

William Hutton

***

A soldier will fight long and hard for a bit of coloured ribbon.

Napoleon Bonaparte

***

No one ever choked to death swallowing his pride.

Anon.

***

When power leads man toward arrogance, poetry reminds him of his limitations. When power narrows the area of man's concern, poetry reminds him of the richness and diversity of his existence. When power corrupts, poetry cleanses.

John Fitzgerald Kennedy

***

Pride would be a lot easier to swallow if it didn't taste so bad.

Brad Moore

***

In general, pride is at the bottom of all great mistakes.

John Ruskin,

***

PRIDE   119

There is nothing that will kill a man so soon as having nobody to find fault with but himself.

George Eliot

***

Take all your dukes and marquesses and earls and viscounts, pack them into one chamber, call it the House of Lords to satisfy their pride and then strip it of all political power. It's a solution so perfectly elegant and preposterous that only the British could have managed it.

Charles Krauthammer

***

Pride perceiving humility honourable, often borrows her cloak.

Thomas Fuller

***

Airs of importance are the credentials of impotence.

Johann Kaspar Lavater

***

Temper gets you into trouble. Pride keeps you there.

Anon.

***

Pride costs more than hunger, thirst and cold.

Thomas Jefferson

***

120   The *Seven Deadly Sins*

Nothing has been purchased more dearly than the little bit of reason and sense of freedom which now constitutes our pride.

Friedrich Nietzsche

***

Idleness and pride tax with a heavier hand than kings and governments.

Benjamin Franklin

***

Of all the causes that conspire to blind Man's erring judgment,
    and misguide the mind,
    What the weak head with strongest bias rules,
    Is pride, the never-failing vice of fools.

Alexander Pope

***

A proud man is always looking down on things and people; and, of course, as long as you're looking down, you can't see something that's above you.

C. S. Lewis

***

Most of the trouble in the world is caused by people wanting to be important.

T. S. Eliot

***

PRIDE 121

Pride and poverty don't get along, but often live together.

Proverb

***

Through pride we are ever deceiving ourselves. But deep down below the surface of the average conscience a still, small voice says to us, Something is out of tune'.

Carl Gustav Jung

***

Pride is the mask of one's own faults.

Jewish proverb

***

Pride is pleasure arising from a man's thinking too highly of himself.

Benedict de Spinoza

***

The sin of pride may be a small or a great thing in someone's life, and hurt vanity a passing pinprick, or a self-destroying or ever murderous obsession.

Iris Murdoch

***

122 The *Seven Deadly Sins*

Pride makes us esteem ourselves; vanity desires the esteem of others.

Anon.

***

It is funny the two things most men are proudest of is the thing that any man can do and doing does in the same way, that is being drunk and being the father of their son.

Gertrude Stein

***

The infinitely little have a pride infinitely great.

Voltaire

***

I would not talk so much about myself if there were anybody else whom I knew as well.

Henry David Thoreau

***

Thus unlamented pass the proud away,
　　The gaze of fools and pageant of a day;
　　So perish all, whose breast ne'er learn'd to glow
　　For others' good, or melt at others' woe.

Alexander Pope

***

Pride (of all others the most dang'rous fault)
   Proceeds from want of sense, or want of thought.

Wentworth Dillon

***

A father's pride, laid on thick, has always made me wish that the fellow had at least experienced some pain during procreation.

Karl Kraus

***

We should be ashamed of our pride, but never proud of our shame.

Anon.

***

Wounded pride can take a rich young man far who is surrounded by flatterers since birth.

Stendhal

***

And the Devil did grin, for his darling sin
   Is pride that apes humility.

Samuel Taylor Coleridge

***

124   The *Seven Deadly Sins*

Search well and be wise, nor believe that self-willed pride will ever be better than good counsel.

Aeschylus

***

Some people are proud of their humility.

Henry Ward Beecher

***

Pride goeth before destruction, and an haughty spirit before a fall.

Bible, Proverbs

***

Pride is like the beautiful acacia, that lifts its head proudly above its neighbor plants--forgetting that it too, like them, has its roots in the dirt.

Christian Nestell Bovee

***

Yes - the same sin that overthrew the angels,
    And of all sins most easily besets
    Mortals the nearest to the angelic nature:
    The vile are only vain; the great are proud.

Lord Byron

***

Pride breakfasted with plenty, dined with poverty, and supped with infamy.

Benjamin Franklin

***

Pride that dines on vanity, sups on contempt.

Anon.

***

Vanity and pride sustain so close an alliance as to be often mistaken for each other.

Rt. Hon. William Ewart Gladstone

***

How poor a thing is pride! when all, as slaves,
    Differ but in their fetters, not their graves.

Alfred Daniels

***

The disesteem and contempt of others is inseparable from pride. It is hardly possible to overvalue ourselves but by undervaluing our neighbours.

Edward Hyde, Lord Clarendon

***

126   The *Seven Deadly Sins*

The pride of the heart is the attribute of honest men; pride of manners is that of fools; the pride of birth and rank is often the pride of dupes.

Charles Pineau Duclos

***

To lordlings proud I tune my lay,
　　Who feast in bower or hall;
　　Though dukes they be, to dukes I say,
　　That pride will have a fall.

John Gay

***

Deep is the sea, and deep is hell, but pride mineth deeper; it is coiled as a poisonous worm about the foundations of the soul.

Martin Farquhar Tupper

***

Pride, where wit fails, steps in to our defence, and fills up all the mighty void of sense.

Alexander Pope

***

He that is proud eats up himself. Pride is his own glass, his own trumpet, his own chronicle; and whatever praises itself but in the deed, devours the deed in the praise.

William Shakespeare

***

When flowers are full of heaven-descended dews, they always hang their heads; but men hold theirs the higher the more they receive, getting proud as they get full.

Henry Ward Beecher

***

Pride eradicates all vices but itself.

Ralph Waldo Emerson

***

As soon as there was two there was pride.

John Donne

***

Pride makes us artificial and humility makes us real.

Thomas Merton

***

128   The *Seven Deadly Sins*

All other passions do occasional good; but when pride puts in its word everything goes wrong.

John Ruskin

***

A falcon, towering in her pride of place,
    Was by a mousing owl hawked at and killed.

William Shakespeare

***

If he could only see how small a vacancy his death would leave, the proud man would think less of the place he occupies in his lifetime.

Ernest Wilfrid LeGouve

***

Pride is as loud a beggar as want, and a great deal more saucy. When you have bought one fine thing, you must buy ten more, that your appearance may be all of a piece; but it is easier to suppress the first desire than to satisfy all that follow it.

Benjamin Franklin

***

Many men nourish a pride which urges them to conceal their struggles and show themselves only as conquerors.

Honore de Balzac

***

Charity feeds the poor, so does pride; charity builds an hospital, so does pride. In this they differ: charity gives her glory to God; pride takes her glory from man.

Francis Quarles

***

Pride, like laudanum and other poisonous medicines, is beneficial in small, though injurious in large quantities. No man who is not pleased with himself, even in a personal sense, can please others.

Frederick Saunders

***

Pride is increased by ignorance; those assume the most who know the least.

John Gay

***

To be proud and inaccessible is to be timid and weak.

Jean Baptiste Massillon

***

Pride is a vice, which pride itself inclines every man to find in others, and to overlook in himself.

Samuel Johnson

***

130   The *Seven Deadly Sins*

Man, proud man, drest in a little brief authority, most ignorant of what he's most assur d, glassy essence, like an angry ape, plays such fantastic tricks before high heaven, as make the angels weep.

William Shakespeare

***

Pride seems to be equally distributed; the man who owns the carriage and the man who drives it seem to have it just alike.

Henry Wheeler Shaw

***

In beginning the world, if you don't wish to get chafed at every turn, fold up your pride carefully, put it under lock and key, and only let it out to air upon grand occasions. Pride is a garment all stiff brocade outside, all grating sackcloth on the side next to the skin.

Edward George Earle Lytton Bulwer-Lytton, 1st Baron Lytton

***

Pride, where wit fails, steps in to our defence, and fills up all the mighty void of sense.

Alexander Pope

***

It may do good; pride hath no other glass
  To show itself but pride, for supple knees
  Feed arrogance and are the proud man's fees.

William Shakespeare

***

What a lesson, indeed, is all history and all life to the folly and fruitlessness of pride! The Egyptian kings had their embalmed bodies preserved in massive pyramids, to obtain an earthly immortality. In the seventeenth century they were sold as quack medicines, and now they are burnt for fuel! The Egyptian mummies, which Cambyses or time hath spared, avarice now consumeth. Mummy is become merchandise.

Edwin Percy Whipple

***